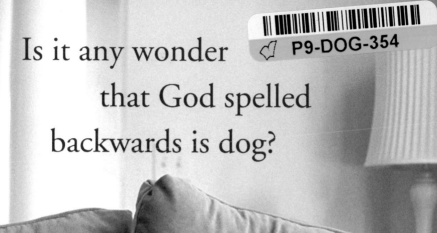

Is it any wonder that God spelled backwards is dog?

conversations with

dog

an uncommon dogalog
of canine wisdom

conversations
with

Dog

an uncommon dogalog
of canine wisdom

Kate Solisti-Mattelon

Council Oak Books
San Francisco / Tulsa

Also by

Kate Solisti-Mattelon

Conversations with Cat

Conversations with Horse

The Holistic Animal Handbook

Kinship with the Animals

Council Oak Books, LLC
San Francisco / Tulsa
www.counciloakbooks.com

Photo credits:
© Brian G. Green / GETTY IMAGES. © Patrice Mattelon page xi.
Photodisc / PUNCHSTOCK pages 1, 5, 11, 15, 57, 73, 85. Brand X
Pictures / PUNCHSTOCK page 43. CORBIS page 99. © Mike Brinson /
GETTY IMAGES page 111.

Cover and interior design by Buffy Terry
Typesetting by Vanessa Perez

Printed in Canada

First printing 2004

Library of Congress Cataloging-in-Publication Data

Solisti-Mattelon, Kate.
  Conversations with dog : an uncommon dogalog of canine wisdom /
Kate Solisti-Mattelon
      p. cm.
  ISBN 1-57178-156-0
  1. Dogs—Behavior—Miscellanea. 2. Human-animal communication—
Miscellanea. I. Title.
  SF433.S627 2004
  636.7—dc22
                                                    2004014433
  ISBN 1-57178-156-0

Acknowledgments

With deepest gratitude to Fiorino and the Council of Canines for giving me the honor of sharing their wisdom and great gifts. And to all canines everywhere who love us and believe in us, no matter what.

Thanks to everybody who wonders what their dogs are thinking and took the time to send me their questions.

Special thank yous to Buffy Terry and Vanessa Perez for designing this beautiful book.

Thanks to all at Council Oak Books for loving this book.

To Patrice, my husband, my soul mate. Thank you for sharing this incredible journey!

To the dogs who have shared (and helped shape) my life so far, Tipsy, Mandy and Mollie. And to the countless dogs I've met through my work who have touched and inspired me. Thank you for all your indescribable gifts to humanity at large, to me, those you love and to the planet!

Contents

- -

In memory of Mollie

She was my lighthouse through the greatest changes and transitions of my life (so far). Thank you, sweet dog, for giving me courage, joy, endless love, and unconditional acceptance. Thank you for teaching me how to trust. I hope you're looking down on me and feeling pleased with my progress. I promise to keep up the "good work."

Thank you for teaching me what it's like to love like a dog. If I can actually do it, well then I've really become a human being!

Animals were once, for all of us, teachers. They instructed us in ways of being and perceiving that extended our imaginations, that were models for additional possibilities.

—Joan McIntyre, *Mind in the Waters*

introduction

As I begin the joyous task of writing this book, my dog Mollie rests at my feet under the desk. Mollie has been with me since 1992 when I adopted her from the Espanola Animal Shelter. She's part Sheltie, part Corgi, with perhaps a little northern New Mexico shepherd mix thrown in for good measure. I call her our designer dog, one of a kind.

What does this being bring to my life and to the lives of my family, friends, and students? She is ever by my side. She sleeps under our bed at night. She sits in on classes, phone consultations, and visits from friends. She chooses to be with her people at every opportunity. Her only alone time is spent eating bones in the backyard or sleeping in a little nest she makes for herself in a sunny spot. She greets most strangers with warmth and happiness. She lives to have her tummy rubbed. Out for a walk, her beautiful tail waves like a little flag, reminding me of all the joy she finds in a beautiful smell-filled excursion. She brings us sweetness, fun, companionship, trust, peace, and calm. Mostly, she brings us love, and love is the reason that I am writing this book.

Why *Conversations with Dog?* Today many people are reading books like, *Conversations with God, Bringers of the Dawn, Angels Among Us,* and *Talking with the Soul.* We are all hungry for wisdom, universal truths, deeper understanding of the purpose of life, and guidance about living balanced lives in harmony with our own purpose and the rhythms of the planet. For years I have been telling people that lying at our feet, curled up at the foot of our beds, or munching in our pastures, are beings who can teach us everything we are seeking. We have only to learn how to open ourselves to hear what they have to tell us.

The kind of communication that I describe in this book goes beyond the physical limitations of instincts, brain waves, mental capacity, and what behavioral scientists have learned or observed about dogs. I am not interested in proving that canine consciousness as I've experienced it is possible as measured by human standards. This book is about tapping into the Divine Consciousness that operates through every creature, plant, stone, and body of water on our planet.

It is my belief that each unique species and individual expresses Divine Consciousness in his or her own way. In this book, I approach dogs through this shared spiritual medium. Though we may express ourselves in different ways, all beings share Divine Consciousness, which is one of the many ways we accomplish interspecies communication and understanding. I don't presume that the information which came to me here is definitive for all time and all canines. I am a vehicle for this information and I have my own filter system. I'm only as good a receiver as my consciousness at this moment allows. As with most information we humans share with one another, the final proof of its usefulness comes through testing it against our own life experiences.

Conversations with Dog is designed to introduce readers to the spiritual, physical, emotional, and mental awareness inherent in the canine species. Individual levels of awareness vary from dog to dog.

Conversations with Dog is not designed to be a manual of any sort. It is a tool for deeper understanding.

It is my hope that books such as *Conversations with Dog, Conversations with Cat,* and *Conversations with Horse* can help people remember how to tap into the Divine Consciousness in dogs, cats, horses, canaries, mice, ferrets, snakes, elephants—all of Creation, animal, vegetable, and mineral—and thus share our experiences once again, as ancient legends say it was intended. I will continue to encourage and support all kinds of interspecies communications in order to deepen understanding and connection between all beings. For me it's all about Love.

Ancient and indigenous peoples have always respected animals as teachers and healers. When the human race was younger, we learned many lessons and were open to receiving the gifts of our fellow Earthlings from species other than our own. Somewhere along the way, we lost our connection with them and with Mother Earth. We began following self-centered journeys focused on greed and domination. As a result, much of humanity today feels discontented, purposeless, unhappy, unfulfilled, separate, and alone.

Many cultures still tell the stories of the deep connections we once enjoyed with the natural world and how we subsequently became separated and isolated from other species and Mother Earth herself. They tell the story of how the dog chose to stay with humans when humans turned away from the rest of nature. I received the story this way:

Once, in the beginning of time, there existed a council of all beings. These beings represented different expressions of the Creator in all sorts of marvelous forms. At the council table sat insects, birds, reptiles, mammals, marsupials, and humans. Each species incarnated to experience life in form, to learn specific truths and to share these with the others so that together we would all understand ourselves and our Creator better. The bee chose its form to learn how to cooperate with the flowering plants. Elephant chose to be the ears of Mother Earth and to experience vibration in the land and air. Cheetah chose to explore and experience speed and grace. Humans examined the gifts they had received and chose to explore their remarkable intellect and the gift of spoken language.

In the beginning, everyone was connected. They were one. They enjoyed sharing their experiences and new understandings of living in form. Then one day, in the pursuit of the mind, we humans stopped returning to the council fire. We became self-absorbed, forgetting that we had agreed to return to the others to share our experiences with them. The chasm between humans and the other creatures of the Earth deepened. Most of the animals continued on their paths, but three species lingered, saddened by the ever-widening gap between humans and animals. At a critical moment, these three made a conscious choice to join their purpose and evolvement with human beings. They consciously chose to leave the comfort of their fellow creatures to a great extent and accompany the humans, hoping to lead us back to Source, back to connection, back to Love. These three species were the dog, the cat, and the horse. Even to this day, we have only to stop and pay attention and these three will remind us of who we truly are.

I chose to start this exploration of our relationships with other beings with the dog since this, more than other species, has been part of our human family the longest. A few years ago, scientists believed that the dog had been domesticated for around 14,000 years. Recently, genetic evidence has been discovered which indicates that canines have been with us for perhaps 130,000 years. From that long-ago time up through today, the original wolf dog has developed into an unbelievable variety of forms, from the Teacup Poodle, weighing in at two-and-a-half pounds to a 180-pound Alaskan Malamute! Amazingly, the DNA of these divergent breeds, as well as every breed in between, share most of the wolf's DNA.

In English, dog spelled backwards is god. The coincidence is not lost on many of us. Look at the qualities we ascribe to our benevolent god-mercy, patience, forgiveness, unconditional love. Look at the qualities of dog-loyalty, devotion, unconditional acceptance, forgiveness, patience. Our dogs teach us about unconditional love by role-modeling it for us daily.

Perhaps if we ask, they will teach us how we too can be this way.

where do we look
for answers to our
questions ?

chapter one

"*Dogs are the most amazing creatures; they give
unconditional love. For me they are the
role model for being alive.*"
—Gilda Radner, *It's Always Something*

Most of us look to human teachers for guidance about how to live our lives and be happy. Some of us look to ancient and modern books, carvings and manuscripts, seeking explanations of the heavenly truths, which are somehow perceived as better than earthly wisdom. Gratefully, throughout history, humans have been graced with extraordinary human teachers, masters, saints, and sages. It stands to reason that enlightened humans would have answers for the rest of us. No matter how brilliant or evolved these human teachers may be, they are still human. How vast can their perspectives be unless they learn to tap into other wisdoms, other perspectives?

Today, we are willing to travel halfway around the world, and even to learn other people's languages, in order to explore other realities. Yet, most of us don't think twice about what an animal or group of animals might think or care about. What if we each had the ability to tap into perspectives other than human ones? Wouldn't that contact broaden our perspectives and understanding? Just as we've learned to speak each other's human languages, we can learn the languages of non-human beings, providing us the opportunity to explore their ways of seeing the world. What could we learn if we opened our minds and our hearts to other non-human realities? Is it perhaps possible for us to find our sacred humanity by understanding how animals perceive us and for us to know more about our connection to them and to the planet? I believe the answer to that question is yes. I think many of us are ready.

Are you?

Maybe you're feeling skeptical about communicating with animals, but think about it. Those of us who love animals and live with them are experiencing interspecies communication all the time. Look at your dog. Think of all the subtle and not-so-subtle messages the two of you exchange. You read his body language all

What special language do you and your dog share?

the time. A wagging tail, a joyful bark, downcast eyes, pawing at your pant leg, a scratch at the door, a tilt of the head, a lick on the face. All of us understand this communication. Many of us learn to read more subtle, personal signals as well, such as a cocked head and quizzical look when our animal friends are trying to understand us, or an excited wiggle of their behind when we pick up the car keys to go for a ride.

People have shared wonderful stories with me about the unusual ways their dogs get their points across. Start paying more attention to the unique signals your dog sends you and you will begin to see how good animals really are at letting us know their needs.

Many people speak to their dogs in funny voices, creating a special form of communication between human and dog. What is the special language you speak to your dog?

What do you see in your dog that is different from other dogs you have lived with or known?

Think about special canine friends you have known. What made them special?

So now that you are thinking about how much you and your dog really do understand each other, let's go to the next level. For the sake of exploration, set aside all you've learned about what you can and cannot do. Tell yourself that you actually can communicate with your own dog. Tell yourself that you are receiving information from him all the time and that he understands you as well. If you're struggling with this, ask him if he wants to go for a walk. Did he understand you? Did you understand his response? Of course!

The next step is to observe your dog with the new understanding that you two are communicating all the time.

What do you notice that's different from before?

Is your dog sending you any new signals now that you are paying attention in a different way?

When you touch your dog, be aware of how you are touching her. How does she respond to different strokes, scratches, pressure, speed? What happens when you leave your hand just above her body? Can you see how she feels your hand even though you haven't made physical contact? By closely observing your dog and her responses to you, you are learning to pay attention to subtle communication. With practice, this observation will develop into deeper awareness. Conscious touch with clear, simple communication can lead you to develop your connection with your dog into a beautiful partnership. Love combined with all of the above will lead you into understanding yourself and the essence of Dog.

earthly beings with *cosmic* understanding

chapter two

"We humans should never forget our capacity to connect with the collective spirit of animals. Their energy is essential for our future growth."

-Shirley MacLaine, *Dancing in the Light*

We are reading a lot about messages from angels, spirit guides, ascended masters, and even our own souls. What do these beings have in common with dogs? What are the differences? To start with the obvious, dogs are physical beings, the others are not. This means that dogs experience pleasure, pain, taste, smell, sight, temperature, hunger, thirst, hormonal impulses, youth, maturity, old age, birth, life, and death. We humans experience all these things as well. The angels, our souls, or higher selves, and spirit guides do not experience these things.

Dogs are aware of their connection to God. Unlike most humans, they have never forgotten or lost it. The angels, ascended masters, and even our own souls, know this oneness with God and all other beings. We humans are desperately trying to remember.

Ah ha! So you see, dogs are in a unique position. They share our physical reality and know and live every moment of every day in a oneness that we are struggling to know! Do they know that they know? I say, emphatically, YES! Let me share a story with you about the dog's mission and how our lives are intertwined:

Years ago I was working with a woman who wished to create a healing system for animals. This woman was motivated to do this work by a remarkable Italian Greyhound who shared her life for many years. This unusual dog had broken all the rules of what the woman thought she knew and understood about human/canine relationships. This wonderful dog had changed the woman and awakened her to her life's purpose. As a result, the woman honored the animal's gifts to her by creating a healing system for veterinarians and other practitioners to use in cooperation with the animals in their care. In order to create this system, she wanted to go beyond what human beings thought they knew about

Dogs are aware of their connection to God.

what animals need. She wanted to ask the animals themselves what they needed. To do this she sought the assistance of a person capable of tapping into animal consciousness.

The woman knew she had to test the information received from this person who was going to help her so that she could feel confident that this person was indeed receiving credible information from the animals. The way to test the person was to see how she connected with the Italian Greyhound. What could the psychic tell her about her dog? Well, as it turned out, the psychic could tell her almost everything. By receiving information that only the dog and his person knew, the woman felt confident to pursue her work with the animal communicator. Together they created a triangle—the woman, the psychic animal communicator, and the dog.

When they asked the dog what all dogs wanted or needed in order to be whole, well and happy, the answer was a surprise. The dog spoke through the psychic and told the humans the dog's mission in life. He said that in order for a dog to be whole, well, and happy, he/she needed to fulfill his or her mission. Here is the mission, described with simplicity and beauty:

The mission of all dogs is to bring unconditional love to humanity through the qualities of loyalty, devotion, and complete acceptance. The canine species has freely chosen to be bred into a variety of shapes and sizes in order to be at the side of humans in all walks of life—from the hunting hounds of a king, to a shepherd's herding dog, to a lady's lap dog. By accompanying human beings on their different life journeys, the dog can spread unconditional love worldwide.

Everything a dog does, he does to demonstrate love to his person. The German Pointer helps his master hunt birds. The Saint Bernard rescues lost hikers. The Scottish Terrier guards home and hearth. The Chihuahua catches mice and watches for intruders. The Keeshound guards the merchant's goods on the barge. The Basset Hound hunts badgers. The Maltese lives to be in physical contact with his person, seeking out laps and pillows. The Collies and Shepherds herd sheep and protect the shepherd's family, and so on. Although they do all sorts of jobs, these marvelous beings have one purpose in mind, to model unconditional love.

We humans think that we have bred the dog for different tasks. In fact, the dog has agreed to be bred to be near us, and to succeed brilliantly at what we need them to help us do. We humans, with our emphasis on "doing," have come to believe that the purpose of the dog is to do, not to be. Wrong. Can you see that your own dog's highest purpose is to be with you? Sure, some retrievers live to play ball. Some even play ball by themselves. But observe this dog's energy and body language when she plays alone versus when her person enters into the game. I guarantee it is different. It is this emotional and spiritual connection that brings the dog joy, for it is here that she fulfills her mission and purpose.

So, if the divine purpose of the canine species is to perpetuate unconditional love, isn't it a good idea to examine how they do this and what they have to say about living all the time in a state of unconditional love?

DOG'S TEACHING STARTS WITH OUR PAYING ATTENTION

How do we learn to be present in our lives? So many of us are frustrated by feelings of the same old grind, nothing new or interesting in our lives, a sense of wanting more. Most human beings live in the past, prisoners of their experiences with their parents, teachers, bosses. Others of us live only in the future. I'll meet the mate of my dreams some-

Dogs are fully present in the moment.

day. I'll buy that dress tomorrow. I'll have the job I want later. I'll spend time with my children next week. What if I don't have enough? What if she gets angry with me? When we live in the past or the future, we become completely disconnected from the present. Life passes us by. We search for happiness instead of creating it now. As long as something is being searched for, worked toward, it is never here. Dogs are fully present in the moment. They don't think about what they had for breakfast once breakfast is finished. They don't worry about what will happen later. They are enjoying this present moment which will be a new moment in a second.

Are you living in the past or in the future? Observe how you speak. Are you just repeating things you learned to say, or do you mean what you say? Do you use phrases like, "I will have lots of money someday"? Notice that someday is never today. Take a lesson from dog; try shifting the way you speak, incorporating present tense where you once used future tense. Try saying, "I have all the money I want and need right now." Do this enough and the universe will soon catch up.

Dogs understand this. Notice how one dog focuses on your sandwich. He isn't thinking, "Gee, it would be nice if you gave me that sandwich." He's thinking instead how good that sandwich tastes RIGHT NOW.

To pay attention and be fully present in life is to use all the gifts you have been given. Use all your senses, including your feelings: taste, smell, feel, listen, and see. Breathe! Do you choose to experience beauty? Do you choose to experience ugliness? Do you wish to have fun while you're alive or do you stick to drudgery? It's your choice and the dog in your life can be a most valuable teacher. Are you willing to take responsibility for creating your own life? If you are, let your dog show you how to LIVE!

So, if your dog were talking to you now, what would you see, hear, feel? What would you experience?

life
according
to dog

chapter three

"I believe that animals have been talking to
human beings ever since we were all made
and put into this world."
—Barbara Woodhouse, *Talking to Animals*

Once we believe that we can understand what our dogs are communicating to us, we can begin to hear their thoughts. I was able to hear the thoughts of animals and plants when I was a very young child. I thought this was normal. I quickly learned that my parents did not think it was normal at all! By age eight, I closed down the parts of myself that knew how to listen. Then, in my late twenties, I decided to take responsibility for my life and stop blaming my parents, my job situation, the weather, and other external conditions, for all that happened to me. I began to pay attention to my everyday choices. I began to listen to my heart. I began to make new choices. I asked for help and guidance. I read self-help books. My therapist was a big help. In therapy, while seeking self-knowledge, I discovered pieces of myself that had been locked away from me. I became aware that I had filed away the feminine, intuitive parts of my consciousness and had replaced them with qualities that society valued more—assertiveness, accomplishment, doing, doing, doing. As I began integrating these missing parts, something miraculous happened. I began to feel nature differently. I began to sense even more than the physical plants and trees, rocks, and water. I became aware of something more. I felt joy, peace, and oneness.

As I allowed myself more time to be in nature and to do nothing, I began to hear the trees talking to me. The feeling was amazing, so peaceful, so kind, so loving. I knew that I wasn't nuts because I had learned to trust myself and my feelings when they felt right. I continued to explore my growing awareness and surrendered to the listening. Eventually, I was able to hear all of nature, animals, birds, water, and rocks.

Dogs have been some of my greatest teachers.

This experience led me to a profound connection with the Earth. I believe that I woke up and remembered my connection to the Divine Consciousness in all living things. I know now that I am connected to all living things and that we are all a part of God. I know this beyond a shadow of a doubt.

I feel honored whenever I can give other humans the opportunity to connect in the ways I am describing. My husband, Patrice, and I have dedicated our lives to helping people create connection, first with themselves and later with the animals and nature around them. It is my great joy to share the Divine wisdom of the animals with those who are ready to listen. Since dogs have been some of my greatest teachers, I bring their wisdom to you in this format, with the hope that you will learn to seek out and respect their tremendous gifts and learn to listen and live the lives God has given us all. Have Fun!

GETTING STARTED

What questions would we ask our dogs? The best place to start is often with the most obvious questions that I have heard people ask. If you look deeply, the answers to these mundane questions often hold some surprises.

living with

humans

"*The fidelity of a dog is a precious gift demanding no less binding moral responsibilities than a friendship of a human being. The bond between a true dog is as lasting as the ties of this earth can ever be.*"

—Konrad Lorenz

What is the best way
to speak to dogs?

*Simple, clear, positive
communication is the most effective.*

A: We understand much more than most humans think we
do. We hear your thoughts, read your body language and
your energy field. Your spoken word is only one part of the
communication. The best way to speak with us is with
directness and clarity. Think first about what you want to
tell us. Tell us what you want, not what you don't want. For
example, most of the time we hear, "No, no, no! Don't do
this. Stay off the couch," etc. Your body language and energy field radiate displeasure. We become uneasy, frightened,
upset that we have upset you. Often we don't know exactly
what we've done because you are not always clear. Here's a
better way. Praise us and reward us for the things you wish
us to learn and do. You will be relating to us with joy and
love. We will feel supported and know we're making you
happy. It's okay to tell us not to chew the newspaper, but
give us the chew toy you want us to chew and tell us,
"Good girl, chew this!"

Tone of voice is very important. We associate high-pitched sounds with happy, nervous, or worried communication. We associate strong, direct moderate tones with instruction. We associate low, deep tones as warnings.

Experiment with your voice and notice how we respond. Tell us not to do something in a low, deep tone. Tell us you're happy with something we've done in a high, happy voice. Give commands in a clear, moderate voice. Notice if you're mixing up the three. See how we get confused?

Visualization is very helpful. Since we are always reading your minds, a clear mental picture will insure that we understand your spoken word. Often we are aware that you are thinking one thing and saying another. This is very confusing. If you tell us, "Go get the ball," but you are thinking, "She'll never find it," we receive a mixed message. Depending upon how strong our desire is to please you, many of us will follow your thought over your words as there are usually stronger emotions accompanying the thought.

If you visualize what you want, along with using your voice, it will be much easier for us to understand you. The way to do this is to focus on what you want us to do. Make a picture in your mind of us being completely successful in whatever it is you want us to do. And finally, tell us what you want us to do, using your voice.

It's also important to pay attention to your body language when you talk to us. Is all of you focused in the direction you wish us to go? Is your body or your energy field moving forward when you're asking us to stop? If you are thinking and feeling yourself going on while you are telling us to stop, it is very confusing. Remember, we pay more attention to your thoughts, body, and aura than to your words. Coordinate your thoughts, body, and spoken words together. If you are consistent with this, you will see that we will master complicated instructions very rapidly. You will learn to trust us and we will learn that we can depend on you for clear directions. Everybody will feel great!

What is the biggest obstacle to human-canine communication?

Separation.

A: As long as you see us as separate from you and less-developed in mental capacity, you will never enjoy clear communication. Your belief system colors every relationship you have. Because you believe that interspecies communication is not possible, at least between humans and other creatures, you cannot possibly communicate. But people among you who discard this dreary belief will open up wonderful, exciting worlds that previously were the realm of imagination!

Think about it. Every interesting thing you have created as a species began as an idea. It became a physical reality because someone believed that it could be. You limit yourselves so much. Why? We suppose it's out of fear. It would have to be. So, what are you afraid of? Are you afraid that your neighbor, family, friends, co-workers, teachers will think you are crazy because you entertain the idea that species other than humans have feelings, intelligence, and are spiritual beings? Don't be limited by others' fears and beliefs. Every time one person decides to reject fear, the world becomes a brighter, more loving place. Every time one person breaks away from collective beliefs and embraces a new concept, freedom in all forms is given life and breath.

Communication is an activity of the body, heart, and mind. Communication is connection. When one person accepts that the being she is communicating with is a reflection of herself, a mirror, God smiles. When one person embraces another being as family, God laughs with joy.

Are you offended when we refer to you as our children or refer to ourselves as your mommy or daddy?

Everybody needs somebody.

A: That's not easy to answer. We know that many of you need us to be your children. Many of you need children to feel whole and happy. You need someone to love and care for. Most of us understand that calling us your children is your way of showing how much you love us. Love is perfectly okay, expressed in every way. But you should also know that some of us have come to teach you how to respect us as equals. Ask yourself if it totally serves our partnership to always see us as children. Do you see us as babies? Do you see us as adolescents? Young adults? If we are no longer puppies, it can be hard to be referred to as a baby. When you speak lovingly to us in high, happy tones, the communication makes sense. In our canine communication, we speak lovingly to each other in high, happy tones. If you talk baby talk to us, we assume you are treating us like babies. We might work to fulfill your picture by never really growing up. As long as you speak baby talk we might continue to behave like puppies, chewing on things, peeing when we're excited and whining to get your attention. The question to ask is why do you talk to us this way.

Sometimes your seeing us as babies blocks you from receiving the important gifts we have to give as adults. If you pay attention and ask yourself why you call us children or babies, you may find the holes in your heart. Some of these holes we are happy to fill. Others you must learn to fill yourself. You can build your own home of self-love upon the foundation of love that exists between us. As this home becomes more and more comfortable to you, invite other human beings in to share the warmth it offers. If you lavish all your love on us, we will be disappointed. Our purpose is to help you receive and give love to all beings, including human beings, not just to us.

Do you like it when we tell you that you're pretty, adorable...or we call you pet names that we think are cute?

Everybody loves a compliment!

A: Of course! It is your way of appreciating us and telling us that you love us. Occasionally we get embarrassed if you pour it on too much. Some of us who consider ourselves to be regal, majestic, or elegant might not like being called cute. If you observe how we carry ourselves in the world and honor us for who we are, you'll always choose the words that fit us best.

Do you like to be kissed?

*A human kiss is different
from a canine kiss.*

A: It all depends on the energy behind the kiss and our personal experiences with people being close and personal like that. If a person we love and trust comes to kiss us, normally we are happy about that. If a person comes in too fast, like when they blow in our faces, it feels invasive and we draw away or maybe even snap if we are uncomfortable. If a person is really needy and kisses us because they need our love, we will usually tolerate it but not really enjoy it. Remember, your human idea of kissing is very different from ours. Canine kissing always includes a wet tongue! If you licked us in the face, like we enjoy doing to you, we'd understand completely what you are expressing. No translation needed! Most of us have to learn how to receive human kisses. Fortunately, we readily understand the love behind the kiss, so quickly we learn to translate.

Do your emotions change when mine do, supporting or mirroring me?

We remind you of how joyful life really is.

A: Sometimes we choose to mirror your emotions in order to help you see yourself and your choices. Other times we sense that you need to be reminded how joyful life truly is. When you're really down in the deepest darkness, we feel it is important to help you find the light. To that end we might get silly, drag out our toys, the leash, whatever, to help you move your body, laugh, shift the energy, and remember that as long as you pay attention to the dog in your life you won't be able to stay sad for long.

What do you taste when you lick me?

Licking is one of the ways we greet family members.

A: It is equivalent to a human kiss. We lick you to signal affection, to get your attention, or just to express our love for you. Each of you tastes differently, but we never confuse your taste with the taste of food, unless there's something wrong with us. Sometimes we'll lick your hand after you've touched a delicious food. Sometimes we lick you to clean you. Sometimes we lick you to help you calm down. Sometimes we get obsessive about licking. This usually signals an emotional imbalance. Perhaps we're lonely or feeling purposeless or bored. Eventually this type of licking becomes a bad habit. If you feel our licking is too much, ask us what we are trying to communicate to you. Look to see if loneliness or boredom could be the cause.

Sometimes our licking you is not to tell you that we have a problem but a way of drawing your attention to your own emotional problem. We might be trying to get you to look at your own loneliness, boredom, or lack of fulfillment. Perhaps you are in need of more loving touch, kisses, and affection. Think about this if we are licking you a lot, and look at these possibilities.

Why do you like some people, but obviously dislike others?

We're good judges of character.

A: When we come in contact with your energy field, we clearly read your likes, desires, motivations. When a person has anger, threatening intentions, or fear, we might respond with a defensive attitude or even with aggressive action. This is why so many of you recognize that we are excellent judges of human character. Beyond perceiving an unspoken threat from a person, we are drawn to certain energies and repelled by others, just as each of you are. We rarely choose to be around a person whose energies clash with ours as this clash will make it difficult or impossible to create a relationship built on unconditional love.

However, sometimes we push ourselves on those of you who dislike us because we know you need our love most of all! We know that your soul is in harmony with ours even when your personality thinks otherwise.

Why do some of you choose to stay with owners who mistreat you or train you to fight?

You must understand our mission.

A: Because we have agreed to accompany you on your journeys, we are often at your mercy, so to speak. We agreed to be bred to help you, but some people abuse this sacred trust and use us as they use others of their own species. These people are out of balance, lonely, and confused. Beings who consciously engage in cruelty for any reason have lost their way. They are not humane and are not living by the principles all of your religions hold dear. They have forgotten what love really is.

Our mission is service, but often, because of human pain and greed, this mission gets distorted. Through selective breeding we will manifest the same traits as our abusers. We will become disconnected and lost. We will not know that we can change our situations. We are literally stuck—physically and spiritually, just as these humans are. Some of us get a glimpse of love and make a break for freedom. But if we're an escaped Pit Bull or fighting dog looking for love, euthanasia is often our only reward.

Remember, if you can't accept us, and you feel that you must euthanize us, the best way to help us break free of the cycle of abuse is to send us to the arms of God with all the love you can muster. Don't numb yourselves or feel pity, anger, or sadness at the time of our passing, or we will likely return with that energy. You have the ability to help us break free. Never forget that love is the answer to ending the cycle of abuse.

*I*f you love your human family, why do you run away sometimes?

We are descended from wolves.

A: Our ancient blueprint includes a great deal of wandering. We're built to wander miles in search of food if necessary. Some of our brothers and sisters have what you would call a "wander lust." Huskies have a deep need for freedom. Our wolf-memory, as well as being bred as sled dogs, means that we crave wandering and need freedom from time to time. No fence, electric or otherwise, can keep us in if we have to get out. Those people who love and understand us respect our need for freedom and do their best to provide it. Also, we remind human beings about the importance of wandering freely from time to time. Everybody needs a walkabout sometimes!

Occasionally we need a break from the demands of family life. We need to run or wander to get exercise, explore, feel the wind in our ears—to be totally free for a moment. It's selfish, to be sure, but it helps us reconnect to the Earth. Afterwards we are able to recommit to our human family. Sometimes wandering or running away separates us from our people in a way that does not serve you or us. If we get too involved in relating to nature, we reconnect to our more wild selves. This can distract us from our mission with our people and put us in an in-between place, a place between human society and wildness. We can become feral. Then, sometimes we get lost in a spiritual sense as well. Our mission is to be a part of the human journey, not separate from it. Usually the love of a committed person will reach us and return us on track.

Each of us must choose our own balance between responsibility and freedom.

Connection makes a big difference.

A: That depends on many things, such as whether or not we feel comfortable being alone. Again, we are social beings. We are used to being with others of our kind or in human families. Being alone isn't natural or easy for any of us. Some of us become really depressed. Others develop separation anxiety in all different forms. Some of us get sad and quiet. Others panic and become destructive. Some of us get used to being alone, but it is never desirable unless we temporarily need to rest or recuperate.

Past experience also affects how we handle being alone. If we have been left and neglected by a previous person we were with, being alone will stir up the old memories. If we have been overwhelmed by too much stimulation, being alone could be a nice break. However, once we're rested and confident in our new home, we will usually want to be with people or other dogs.

Most of us do much better when we have a companion to keep us company. Being with another dog is usually our first choice. But we can learn to appreciate the company of a sympathetic cat, bird, ferret, turtle, snake, or even a guinea pig. Just as it is important to keep connected to us when you travel, it is important to keep connected with us when you go away for the day. Think of us with love and joy during the day and we will pick up your love and appreciate the connection. If before, during or after you walk out the door you feel separation anxiety, guilt, or sadness, you will reinforce or even create those same feelings in us. On the other hand, if you are upbeat, clear, positive and decisive as you leave, we will feel supported and positive.

Our sense of duty is also a factor when we are left alone. Those of us who are working breeds have a keen sense of duty or responsibility. If you tell us that our job is to guard the house and be sure it remains just as it is when you walk out the door, we will have something important to do while you are away. Some of us really need you to assign us a job while you are away, while others are happy to sleep. All of us have a strong watchdog instinct, some more than others. After all, being the watchdog was one of the main reasons people wanted us to be part of their families and tribes. Be clear with what you want us to do. Tell us what you want, like, "Stay on the floor or on you own bed. Chew your toys or bones." Please don't tell us, "Stay off the couch," or, "Don't eat the remote control." If you put it that way, we will just focus on the couch or how interesting it would be to munch on the remote control.

Tell us when you will be home. Tell us what we will do together when you return.

What can you expect when you come home? Clearly, if the daily routine includes a nice walk or playtime when you come home from work, we really look forward to your return. We're not anxious but excited. If you come home tired and worn out, wanting peace and quiet, but we're all rested and ready to play, we'll both be unhappy in the long run. One or both of us needs to make a change in our schedules to get on the same wave length. Hopefully you're willing to align your needs with ours.

How do you feel about aiding blind, deaf, or disabled people?

It can bring great fulfillment.

A: Normally aiding humans in need is our greatest joy. It's important to know that certain individual dogs are better at aiding disabled humans than others. Different dogs have different gifts. You recognize that Labradors and German Shepherds are generally best suited to help blind, deaf, and disabled people, although many mixed breeds, as well as other individuals, are wonderful helpers, too. The key to success is matching individual dogs to individual humans. Most disabled people with helper dogs love and appreciate their canine partners. However, there are some people who claim that they want a helper dog, then when they have a dog they take out all their frustrations and anger on her. This is a great tragedy for all involved.

People involved in training and placing assistance dogs need to be clear about what they are arranging. Are you training the dog to be a servant or a partner to the human? Do you carefully screen humans to be sure they will be kind to their dog? A dog trained for this type of service has agreed to take on a huge responsibility, an advanced level of service. If she fails, she will probably carry that memory of failure for a long time, perhaps lifetimes. Failure is perceived when the dog is taken from the person they're supposed to help. If someone does not explain to the dog why she was taken from the person, nine times out of ten, she will assume that she failed. Some dogs do not recover from this sense of failure. As someone involved in training or placing assistant dogs, your commitment to mutual respect and partnership can make the difference between a life of misery and a life of joy for both dog and human. This understanding will create far more successful placements and mutually beneficial relationships.

Human beings with disabilities are great and powerful souls who have chosen a difficult physical experience in order to learn and grow in ways that people without physical disabilities will never know. These disabled beings are not less than non-disabled beings. In many cases they are greater! Their souls understand the challenging and rewarding path they have chosen, but often a person's personality gets bogged down with feelings of inferiority, jealousy, victimization, anger, resentment, and frustration. These are obstacles to growth and evolution and, certainly, they feel real and are painful. The dog's job is not simply to aid their person in handling physical challenges but to remind them that they can be more than the pain and frustration. Every day we become role models of compassion, patience, persistence, joy, and love. We remind our person that they are much greater than their bodies. We remind them to be compassionate with themselves. We love you unconditionally, for your spirit and the love that is between us, and the physical disability doesn't affect this love. We help you break through fears of dependency, incapacitation, and sometimes even death. We bring you peace and love. When our person recognizes these gifts, the circle is complete and healing will happen on the most important levels.

Those of you who have chosen this path to train dogs to be with the disabled, or who are involved in placing assistance dogs, have a sacred responsibility to be the facilitator to a life changing and life affirming partnership. Remember this always.

Do you wish to be less reliant on humans, to have more freedom and independence?

A: No, not really. Our destiny is linked with yours. We are in this together, for better or for worse.

How did it happen that dogs and humans would form the kinds of bonds we have today?

It began long, long ago, and in many parts of the world at once.

A: Many peoples the world over chose to have wolf companions, then selectively bred them, with our consent, to help with different jobs. In the deserts of Africa, Greyhounds came into being to help humans hunt. Our bodies were built for speed and to handle the heat. Our narrow heads developed to streamline us as well as to effectively catch and eat small prey, rabbits, rodents, and birds. Our lungs are specialized for running as well. In the cold mountains of Europe, we needed more bulk and fur. Our heads and jaws developed heavier and more squarely than our desert cousins because we were hunting larger animals, like bear, wild boar, and deer. Our bodies developed to fit in with the climate and the prey, as well as to accommodate the job we needed to do.

Why do I love you more than most of the humans in my life?

We're uncomplicated.

A: Our gift to you is unconditional love. We love you no matter how much or little money you make, where you live, what size clothes you wear. With loyalty and devotion, we give you a model of commitment. With absolute trust and uncompromising joy, we show you who you can be. By being the rug beneath your feet which buffers you from all the harshness of life, we help you feel safe in your world. By sending and receiving love, we teach you that you are lovable to others. This is our only agenda.

Most humans have not arrived at this uncomplicated place. Most humans still walk in the world afraid. You are afraid to change, afraid to stay the same. You are afraid to speak for yourselves, afraid to upset the apple cart. You seek prestige and respect, but can't give it to yourself. You collect things in order to fill up an empty space in your heart. As a result of all of this fear and baggage, you create obstacles between yourself and others. Obstacles create separation.

Separation is loneliness. Loneliness is isolation. Separation leads to neediness. Neediness complicates human relationships.

Embrace life as we do and others will enjoy your company. Share love and enjoy each other unconditionally, just as we enjoy you. Live in the moment and make it spectacular. You will begin to find that one fabulous moment connects to another, and another, and another...

you, other dogs,
and other
animals

chapter five

"*Buy a pup and your money will buy love unflinching.*"

—Rudyard Kipling

Why do you bark or snarl at some dogs on our walks, other dogs you're indifferent to, and some you want to play with?

Dog protocol, based on our wolf ancestors' way of walking in the world, has a lot to do with how we act towards one another.

A: Within the wolf pack, each member has a position or status. When we approach each other we send out signals about our status in our family (with you) as well as how we wish other dogs to perceive us. We carry this information in our energy fields. Some of us feel more strongly about asserting our status with other dogs than others do. Usually, those of us who need to be top dog to have the respect of others make a big deal of protocol.

When our energy fields encounter one another, a tremendous amount of information is exchanged. We learn what each other's emotional state is at the moment. We learn what relationship we have with the person we're with. We learn who needs to be dominant, who wants just to play, who is fearful, stressed, unwell, or unhappy. We learn each other's age, breed, and often what we care about—all in a fraction of a second. If our energies are aligned with one another, we'll meet, smell, and decide whether to play or just keep walking. If we feel a conflicting or challenging energy, we will respond physically by sending out warning signals—barking, whining, or snarling and/or lunging for the opponent if we are feeling really uncomfortable or threatened.

Our physical, mental, and emotional states color our perceptions, just as yours do. If we are not feeling well, we can become cranky and edgy with other dogs, even those we seem to like. If we feel that you are uncomfortable with other dogs, we will send out warning signals within our energy fields that can actually attract conflict. Sometimes we do this to prove to you that we can protect you. Other times we do this to keep other dogs away, even if we might enjoy playing with them. Usually, doing our best to help you feel safe is our first priority.

Why do you smell each other's rear ends?

We learn a lot.

A: Dogs have scent glands in the anal area. We use these scent glands to mark our territory, our belongings, whatever we wish. The anal area quickly conveys our sexual interest or disinterest. We can tell what each other has been eating and pooping. We can smell how happy or stressed the other dog is. We can smell their state of health. In short we learn a tremendous amount about each other in a quick sniff.

Are some breeds of dogs meaner than others?

Breeding is a factor.

A: Some of us were originally bred to be fierce guard dogs, fighters, and protectors. Those of us who were bred for these traits use them to protect. Again, none of us are mean by nature. Love and tenderness will be returned in kind. Cruelty will be met by those of us bred to be fierce, with fierce resistance. Are we being mean or just responding with unmistakable clarity?

Our natural instinct is to loyally guard and protect our families—canine and human. If we perceive a threat to someone we love, we usually do something about it. If we are mature, balanced, and healthy, our ability to judge a situation as dangerous or not is excellent. However, if we are trained not to use our own judgment, or if a person trains us to see even the most innocent situation as a life-or-death threat, we can be taught to attack and kill. Our loyalty to the people we have made a bond with becomes the very thing used to manipulate us into harming those we only wish to love.

Sometimes we are turned into killers because we have learned to fear. Usually this is accomplished by a person neglecting and mistreating us. We are not fearful, aggressive, mean, or people killers by nature. People have to train us to be like that. It grieves us deeply to be used in this manner, but unfortunately, until you decide to stop using us to cause harm, we're forced to continue. Remember, we are in service to help you. You have free will and can use your abilities to help or to harm. It's up to you to choose how you wish us to accompany you.

*I*s it true that working breeds are happiest when they work?

Usually this is so.

A: If we were bred to herd sheep or cattle, we feel really good when we do this. If we are a service breed, such as a German Shepherd, Labrador, Saint Bernard, Border Collie, or Rottweiler we have to have a job to do. Lack of structure, boundaries, or useful activity will make a working dog crazy and neurotic. Sometimes this manifests in strange behavior, neediness, or restlessness. Other times it manifests in physical problems such as itching, hot spots, self-mutilation, stomach ailments, inappropriate or difficulties with elimination, destructive behavior. If you aren't willing to give us an important job to do or offer us physical challenges like agility, pick a different breed to share your life with.

There is a variety of jobs we can be happy doing. Some of us require lots of active, physical work. Others will thrive helping people, such as aiding those of you who have disabilities, going to visit people in hospitals, or visiting with old people or children who are in nursing homes. We are good at these tasks because we know and understand what is needed. Make no mistake, those of us who are good therapy dogs are consciously working to comfort and serve you. We know which child needs to gently pat our heads while others want to throw their arms around us, burying happy faces in soft fur. We deliberately give what is needed or required. You can see the result in the faces of those who receive our love.

Some of us are content with simple jobs, especially when we're older. We may be very happy to guard the house while you're gone. The key to helping us feel useful is in asking us to do something for you, and acknowledging our contribution, whatever it is. A simple, "Thanks for taking such good care of the house," accompanied with a pat on the head goes a very long way.

$\mathcal{D}o$ dogs fall in love?

Yes, we do.

A: We are designed to seek out and find the perfect companion, just as you are. In a wolf pack, the alpha pair choose each other for love, strength, and compatibility. They also think about the future of the pack and consider what energy their pups will have. They think about whether or not the blending of their energies will create healthy, balanced offspring. Romantic love is a real thing for us. Sometimes we project our romantic love on to a person when there are no suitable canine partners available. We understand that this will be an unrequited love, as you call it. We know that this type of love is not about procreation, but about true partnership and sharing one heart between two beings.

Why do you howl?

Howling reconnects us.

A: It's a special form of canine expression. Some of us enjoy it more than others. Some of us cannot resist a good howl. Others get embarrassed when people "catch us" howling. It's a personal thing. We howl to connect to other dogs. We howl because it sounds great. We howl in grief sometimes. We howl in loneliness. We howl with happiness. Howling together reconnects us with our pack memories. Our wolf ancestors howled for all these reasons as well as to communicate with all animals within earshot. They howl to remind everybody to be the very best they can be. Part of the wolf's mission is to give us all a model of high integrity. When wolves howl, they get everybody's attention. The sounds they make are magnificent. They speak of integrity, reminding everyone to find, keep, and stand by their own highest calling, no matter what that might be. At one time human beings knew that wolf carried the sacred trust of integrity. If humans devoted themselves to following the path of the wolf, they could be counted on completely and unconditionally, just like wolf.

Why do you chase cats?

If she acts like prey, we have to act as predator.

A: Oh, there are many reasons! Cats are little and they run. For most of us it is nearly impossible not to chase a small animal running from us. Instinct propels us to chase a small running animal because it could be our next meal. Cats who stand their ground and challenge us are often a different matter. They show us that they are willing to fight if necessary. Most of us pause here to decide if it's wise to fight with this ferocious being who is projecting herself to us as a very large foe. Often we will think better of attacking and back away. Once a cat has done this with us, we are usually more respectful of that cat. Other cats will probably have to earn our respect, although some of us will respect all cats because the first cat stood its ground with us, especially if the cat attacked us or tried to.

Sometimes the cat is not afraid of us and runs to play. You can tell that this is the case when at other times the cat is affectionate and comfortable around us. A cat that hides from us or is frightened leads us to believe that she considers us a predator. If she acts as our prey, it is almost impossible for us not to act as her predator.

How can I get you to stop chasing the cat?

Tell us both what you expect and give us positive reinforcement.

A: First you must explain to us that you want the cat and the dog to get along in your house. You must tell us both what you expect. Set rules or boundaries for us and stick to them. We both need cause and effect. For example, tell us, "I wish you to leave the cat alone. So when she is in the room, I expect you to sit at my side." You will have to reinforce this in the beginning. Treats are helpful, as most of us prefer instant food than food that has to be chased and caught! Treats will often distract us long enough for the cat to get away and for us to focus more on you than on the cat. Some of us will have a harder time adjusting than others. We will have to practice this together for us to really change our behavior long term. Also, if this new relationship is to last, the cat also needs to agree to change. Don't expect too much from us as we are not natural friends. Sometimes the best we will be able to do is to live in relative neutrality. Other times, especially if we have been introduced as puppies or kittens, we will develop friendships. The most important thing is for you to tell us both what you want and to help us get there through positive reinforcement.

How does it feel to chase birds or squirrels with no chance of catching them?

Hope springs eternal!

A: We always do our best for the fun of it. For some of us, the joy of the pursuit and the sudden rush of wings as the bird or birds take flight is thrill enough. Some of us would actually be horrified to catch the bird. Others of us mean business! Predators know it takes many tries to catch our quarry. We are built to never give up until we get what we want. We don't feel exactly what you would call disappointment when we fail. We know failing is part of the game. We just keep at it. It's this very persistence that inspires many of you to do the same in pursuit of your dreams and goals. When we inspire you to greatness, we are tremendously happy and fulfilled!

why you are
the way you are

chapter six

"*No matter how little money and how few possessions
you own, having a dog makes you rich.*"
—Louis Sabin

Why do you bark?

Why do you humans speak?
To express yourself.

A: We bark for many reasons. We bark, whine, whimper, to express ourselves, to communicate simple things such as, "I'm hungry. I need to go outside or come inside. I'm frightened. I'm worried. I'm sad. I'm excited. I'm having a great time. Come here. Someone is at the door. Danger. Friend. Foe. Help!" You see, we use our voices whenever we need to get your attention quickly. Sometimes we get locked into barking and cannot stop. Have you ever met a human who does the same, who starts talking and just can't seem to stop?

Often we need help to stop, if an obsession takes hold. Often a barking obsession takes hold because we've been left alone for too long and we are in despair and feeling lonely. Sometimes, we bark because we are bored. Sometimes we bark because we are angry. Sometimes we bark because we think that's what you need us to do so you'll feel safe and protected.

How can I help you to know
that I need you to stop barking?

*Tell us what you want us to do,
not what you don't want.*

A: First, you need to think about why we are barking. Look to see if you are giving us clear messages or mixed messages. For example, if you feel unsafe when the doorbell rings, we will rush to the door to tell whoever is there that we are here to protect you, our person. If you tell us, "No, no, stop barking," but we sense that you are still afraid, we will not understand what is going on with you. If you tell us, (and mean it), "It's okay, I feel safe. Sit down next to me," we will understand much better. Plus, you are telling us what you want us to do, not what you don't want.

Why do you like to roll in smelly stuff?

Rolling in smelly stuff feels great!

A: Smelly stuff? By that you must mean stuff that smells really bad to humans? Well, there's a world of difference between what you think smells bad and what we think smells bad. Let's put it this way, our sense of smell is at least five times more complex than what you humans can smell. For example, if you were to give us a rawhide bone, we may tell you that we can smell the metal that cut the rawhide, the chemicals that treated it, the decay of the skin used to make the bone, the age of the cow, and even sometimes the fear or pain the cow felt as it died. Why would we eat such a thing? Because we were created to eat old, dead stuff and we love to chew.

Rolling in smelly stuff feels great to us. It is sort of like perfume for you. When another dog meets us, they'll smell us plus the great stuff we rolled in and they will share in the great experience that we had!

Why do you have bad breath?

Who says we have bad breath?

A: Just as beauty is in the eyes of the beholder, so it is with bad breath. Because we are carnivores and carrion feeders, our breath is different from yours. What a being eats has a great deal to do with how their breath smells. To us, our breaths smell grand. Have you ever smelled a lion's breath? Or a hyena's? Now they have some odiferous breath! Sometimes our breath is bad because of a sugar imbalance. We're built to eat meat, not cereal. When we eat the right balance of proteins and vegetables, our breath is perfect. You may prefer to smell minty-fresh breath, but that's not how a dog's breath should smell.

However, certain bad breath can indicate problems. We can smell the difference between healthy dog breath and unhealthy dog breath. We can smell the difference between bad breath caused by dental problems and bad breath caused by digestion problems or something else not working right. We could even teach you how to smell each other's breath to detect health problems or imbalances in diet. Our noses are better equipped for this than yours are, but we could learn how to work together to help you identify diseases by smelling a person's breath.

The important point is that there is bad breath and there is bad breath. Learn to tell the difference by getting close. Smell our breath. If it's not too yucky, we are probably just fine. If you smell a change in our breath, a metallic smell, a sickly-sweet smell, we are probably not well. Usually a fast will clear things up if we've eaten something which does not agree with us, but sometimes we'll need help to get back on the path to healthy dog breath.

Why do we always associate dogs with bones?

We are built to get valuable nutrients from bones.

A: This goes back to ancient times when we sat around campfires with our humans. They shared bones with us, especially when we had cooperated with them in the hunt. Because our teeth were better suited to scraping than the humans' teeth, we were able to chew up the bones. Unless humans crushed the bones, they couldn't get to the good stuff inside. We are experts at scraping, crushing, and eating bones. Providing there was enough to go around, people gave us the bones because we could eat them more easily and clean up everything. We're also what you refer to as carrion feeders. This means we are happy to eat dead things. Bones are an obvious part of a partly decayed carcass. We are built to get valuable nutrients from bones.

Why do you bury your bones and sometimes your toys?

Save for a rainy day.

A: Mother Nature taught us to eat what we need, but always try to save a little something for later. It is no problem for us to eat food which has been buried or is not exactly fresh. We are opportunists. We eat lots of things that other animals might pass up. Digging and burying things is deeply encoded in our brains. Those of us bred to hunt creatures who live in burrows are especially fond of digging.

Burying our toys is an extension of burying our food. That way, we always have something fun put away for later. Practicality and fun should always go together.

Why do you shake your toys and growl at them?

We're pretending that the toy is our prey.

A: Shaking a toy such as a stuffed animal or sock is an imitation of the way we kill small prey animals. The shaking breaks the toy's neck, so to speak. We realize that our toy is not a live creature, but it's great fun to imagine! Sometimes you'll see us stalk our toys, growl at them, and then throw them in the air before shaking them to death. This is just play killing and is great fun.

Why do you love socks?

Your socks tell us a lot about you.

A: As you may have noticed, socks carry the distinct odor of your feet. Your feet perspire differently than other parts of your body and that's a smell we associate with you. Actually, we love underwear and tee shirts, too, because they smell wonderful in their own ways. Just as we smell each other's bottoms to learn all about one another, your socks tell us a lot about you. Different odors tell us what foods you've been eating, how stressed you are, and other things about what's going on with you. Socks made from different materials smell differently, too. Because of our love for smelly stuff, the smellier your socks, the better we like them. We like their size and shape as well. A good, smelly sock can be a good substitute for a small dead animal. We like to play like we are killing them by shaking them furiously. Imagination is really helpful for enhancing our enjoyment of a sock!

Is it pure joy that makes you ram and slam through the tall grass?

It's a glorious experience of connecting to life!

A: Every moment holds a fresh, new gift to enjoy. Ramming and slamming through the tall grass engages our bodies and senses together. We reconnect to the plants, the trees, the earth under our four feet. We feel the breeze through our fur and on our skin. It's a glorious experience of connecting to life! Try it sometime. Abandon yourself to a good run through the tall grass. Breathe deeply and smell what it's like to be alive!

Does it feel good when you wag your tail?

It feels great!

A: Wagging a tail is not only an expression of joy, it moves joy through our whole bodies. It's wonderful to feel joy physically moving down our backs. You can do the same by dancing—really letting yourself go into the feeling of joy. Try completely abandoning your whole body to joy and you'll feel what it's like to wag a tail.

Do you see colors?

Yes, of course we do.

A: At one time, humans dissected and examined our physical eyes and decided that we didn't have the physical equipment to perceive color. How little you actually perceived! Remember we see with senses beyond the physical. We can smell color, can you? Color is a vibration, like every physical thing. Red has a distinctly different vibration from blue, or yellow or green. We perceive colors in tremendous variety, dimension and combination. Red, for example is not flat, but rather a rapid, excited vibration combining white, yellow, orange, and sometimes blue, brown, and purple. Sometimes, in your art, you perceive colors as we do. Colors for us are layers of energy interacting in a vibrant, living relationship.

How is it possible for one species—dog—to have such a vast variety of size and shape?

Isn't it fun?

A: We domestic dogs hold the distinction in the animal kingdom of having the greatest variety within our particular family. But remember, from a biological standpoint, even a Teacup Poodle shares DNA with a timber wolf, so technically we're very similar! But looking at us, indeed there is an extraordinary variety.

We have agreed to be bred into all these shapes and sizes to accompany you in every way we can. Also, this incredible variety allows us to have totally different experiences in different shapes and sizes. For example, the experience of a two-pound Poodle is vastly different from that of a one-hundred-pound Malamute, whose experience is totally different from a Chihuahua's or Spaniel's, or Dachshund's. Such different body types allow us to reincarnate into a body that is totally different than our previous incarnation, yet totally the same. Sounds fun, huh?

Why can you enjoy killing your toy or even another creature if your desire is to teach us unconditional love?

We don't love killing, but we do love that which we kill.

A: Never forget that at this moment in our evolution we are still predators. There is no contradiction here for us. It's the way life is for us at this moment in time. Enjoyment of the kill is really about gratitude. We don't love killing, but we do love that which we kill. Once upon a time, humans felt the same way. Now it seems that some of you enjoy killing for killing's sake. This is crazy behavior. A wolf who kills without gratitude is ostracized from the pack if he cannot be brought back into balance and love. Killing without gratitude for the animal and its sacrifice is a sign of great imbalance, an indication of grave sickness in the mind, and a disconnection between body and soul. Those of you with this affliction need vast quantities of unconditional love to help you find your way back to wellness.

How do you tolerate cruelty and mistreatment and still respond with unconditional love?

We can't help it.

A: Again, we are wired to give and receive love. If we can find love, we will choose it. Because we are beings who live in the present moment, our mistreatment can be rapidly replaced with love. Cruelty and mistreatment at the hands of a person indicate that this person is in a great deal of pain. We know that you don't heal pain by withdrawing love. Pain is healed by pouring on more love, and so this is what we do.

other things you
like to do
(or don't)

chapter seven

"*To err is human, to forgive canine.*"

—Anonymous

What is your favorite activity?

We love best what we share
with our people.

A: One of the ways we do this is by engaging them in play. Most people are far too serious. It puzzles us how preoccupied they can become. Humans seem perpetually worried about the past and the future. By engaging you in play, we help you break free of the confines of your mind. We help you get out of your head and back into your physical body. We remind you how to have fun!

As for our favorite activity, that varies from dog to dog, just as it does person to person. There is an old story about a person asking his dog to describe her favorite game. The dog sat quietly and began to think of all the games she loved to share with her person. She thought of chasing sticks. She thought of chasing airplanes. She thought of chasing balls. Each game was as joyful and exciting as the last. But when she told her human this, her human became sad, asking again what the dog liked to do best.

Again the dog could not think of any one thing that was her favorite. Suddenly the dog's human said, "What about when I throw a rock into the stream and you dive for it?"

"Oh, yes, that's it!" the dog replied. "I love that game!" But the truth is that the dog thought that all games were wonderful. The secret was that throwing rocks for her to dive for was her person's favorite game!

Some of us can seem to you to be obsessed with certain activities, like ball playing, for example, or running, digging, or chasing cats or cars. These have a great deal to do with what we have been bred to do. Retrievers were bred to retrieve duck after duck, all day long if necessary. So ball fetching is a natural, especially since most of us no longer fetch ducks for you. The ball has become a substitute for the duck.

Those of us who chase cars or bicycles have a strong need to herd any running creature. For us, a car is like a cow or sheep. Often the need to chase goes back beyond herding to the time we chased down our food. Those of us who dig were usually bred to dig for prey animals in their underground burrows, like rabbits, rodents, badgers, and animals like that.

Do you enjoy obedience
and agility training?

*It depends on the quality
of our partnership.*

A: Obedience training can be a really positive experience or a really negative one. If the trainer is oriented towards encouraging a partnership between people and dogs, and makes learning fun, then it's great! If obedience is about teaching dogs to be subservient and teaching people to be dominant, then it is miserable. Learning obedience in a loving, respectful way is preferable to no training at all. We are happiest when we have structure and boundaries. In a wolf pack, the alpha pair always makes the rules and the boundaries clear. We become insecure, unhappy, and anxious when we have no structure, no boundaries, inconsistent or non-existent rules. Under the tutelage of a caring instructor, obedience training can be a boon to our self-confidence and can help create successful communication between you and us.

Agility training is a wonderful thing for a working dog. Many of us, especially Australian Shepherds, Shelties,

German Shepherds, and Border Collies, thrive in agility work—as long as it's joyful and making you happy. Competition for the sake of competition appeals to very few of us. We know some of you will disagree with that statement, but we ask you to look closer. Look to see if it's really the dog's person who loves competition for competition's sake. If this is the case, then the dog will do her best to make her person happy. So it looks like the dog loves to compete just to compete, but she's really doing it for her person.

Don't go all grumpy on us here. We love to accomplish tasks for you and we love to fully enjoy the beautiful bodies God gives us. The point is that agility work can be joyful and fun. If it's forced, it's not fun for us. Pushing us too hard and destroying the fun will make us quit. When agility is fun, it's great and we will do really well at it.

Remember that we are in-the-moment beings. Some days we just won't be in the mood and we won't get a great score. We don't see agility meets as cumulative. We have no concept of earning points towards a championship. We know that you get very attached to this concept but for us each day on the course is a new day. Today has nothing to do with last Saturday or next Sunday. It's just today. So lighten up and enjoy each day with us. Don't worry about points and titles. They just feed your egos. We love you anyway.

What is the best way to train you?

Focus on creating partnership.

A: Training works best when you enter into it with the attitude of enriching our lives as well as your own. What is the point of the training, after all? Is it about creating a partnership with us? Is it for safety, ours and others? Is it for fun, as in agility training? If training is about dominance and control, you will not have happy, loving companions. If you train us with an attitude of superiority, you will not create partnership.

Communicating clearly is very important, of course. Emphasize the positive and you will have a happy, playful partner. Emphasize the negative and you will create doubt, confusion, disappointment, insecurity.

How much touch you use depends on how you use it. Loving touch is always welcome. Physical punishment, as in hitting us, choking us, jerking our leashes, throwing us on our backs, or kicking us, will create resentment and stubbornness, along with fear and distrust. Show us what you want. For example, when you wish to housebreak a puppy, take her outside and wait for her to do her business. Praise her profusely in high, happy tones. Pet her and love her. She'll get it. Show us with your hand and body how to sit or lie down. Don't push us into position, show us. Respect is key here. Respect and patience. If you give it, you'll receive it!

How do you feel about dog shows?

These are things you need, we don't.

A: Some of us enjoy participating in dog shows because it gives you pleasure when somebody else acknowledges our beauty. Often these shows are very stressful for us, especially when they are held inside and the sounds echo around the room. But as we said about agility competition, we are not interested in earning points or in championships. These are things that you need, we don't. If you are using us to get attention and recognition, then you clearly need more love and attention from us as well. Perhaps it would be a good idea to spend more quality time with us and less time trying to get someone to notice us and you.

*D*o you understand the concept of car? If so, why are so many of you hit and killed by cars?

Cars are a tough concept for many of us to completely grasp.

A: Many of us love to ride in cars, love to watch the world going by at a fast speed, love to go places with you. A stationary car presents an opportunity for going somewhere. A moving car is a different animal all together. Some of us understand that a person is driving the car. Some of us think it moves all on its own like a big cow or sheep. That's why many of us chase cars. Our herding instinct kicks in, and we have to chase the big thing. Very few of us realize that cars are as fast, heavy, and dangerous as they are. If we are injured by a car we've chased, we can learn that it isn't a good idea to continue. However, some of us just can't stop. Our instincts can be stronger than our ability to choose self-preservation or safety. We need to rely on you to keep us safe from moving cars.

It's a good idea to orient us to correct car behavior when we're young. When you take us on walks on the street, keep us away from cars, teaching us to sit when they drive by, or keeping us on the sidewalk with you between us and the street. Never let us run in the street. We will have no concept that it is a danger zone unless you teach us that it is. Most of us trust that the world is a benevolent place with natural obstacles and challenges. Cars are just too fast for most of us to understand and respond to quickly enough.

Inside the car, we need to learn safe behavior. If we jump and bark, we can distract you and cause an accident. If we are in your lap, and you can't do what you need to do to control the car, we both have a problem. Teach us to ride quietly in the back where we will be safe and you will remain focused on the driving.

$\mathscr{D}o$ you like to travel?

Travel means adventure.

A: Remember, our wolf ancestors and most of our cousins, such as coyotes, jackals, and wild dogs, are designed to travel long distances when necessary in search of prey. For us there's a thrill about adventuring into unknown territory. Going places with our human family is enjoyable because the pack is traveling together and we're there to protect you in the new land. Traveling by car is fun for most of us. We can tolerate traveling in a crate on a plane or a train if a reward of shared adventures is the purpose.

$\mathcal{D}o$ you watch television? If so, what type of programs?

It's not the television, it's the togetherness that matters.

A: Mostly we like to be at your side when you watch television. It's usually a great opportunity to get tummy rubs or to lay our heads in your lap or on your finally still feet. If we watch television, we are usually interested in the animals on the screen. But once we recognize that it is only an image, it usually becomes uninteresting for us.

caring
for your body

chapter eight

"All I need to know about dogs is that I love them,
and dogs seem to say to me, 'Okay, you can love me.'
That's it, all of it."

—Joe Garagiola

How can I take better
care of you?

Our needs are simple.

A: We live to serve, love, play. If you love us, you are giving
us what we want and need the most. We need food and
shelter. We need affection, gentle touch, partnership, and
kind words. We need to feel we have a purpose in your life.
We need to feel that we are contributing to the family pack.

Please understand this: many people do not understand
how to feed us, and many of your medicines are very hard
on our systems. Your chemicals are making us sick.
Emotionally we are also challenged because so many of you
are anxious and stressed. One great gift you can give us is
to take better care of yourselves. You see, we are often ill
because we take on your stresses and sometimes your diseases. Our gift of unconditional love to you includes light-
ening your load. We lighten your load by doing our best to
bring you joy and by reminding you how to play. But sometimes we take on your sicknesses.

What can you tell me about what you need to feel nourished?

Nourishment involves many factors.

A: In the beginning times, we were hunter-gatherers, just like humans. We lived together in packs and cooperated in our hunts, just as humans did in your communities. We began our relationship with humanity by first helping out during a hunt. Humans caught on quickly that we had more acute hearing, a better sense of smell, and often a better sense of the game. You learned that you could trust us and began sharing the meal we had helped you catch. In the beginning the hunter, either wolf or human, honored the prey animal we hunted. We acknowledged that the prey animal was giving her life so that we would live. We all lived in a sacred circle—giver and receiver, receiver and giver. We call this the sacred dance between predator and prey. It can be argued that the prey animal is the more evolved being. She chooses to give her life so that others will live. Is this not a great gift? When a hunter is in balance, he has a deep understanding of the gift the prey animal provides and he expresses gratitude to the prey animal before, during, and after each hunt, kill, and meal.

We would do best if our food came from animals who are raised in respectful and loving ways. And we do best when we have a combination of meat, fat, vegetables, and extras like a little grain sometimes.

When you feed us, do so lovingly, for this is how we receive the greatest nourishment.

How can I help you be more comfortable at the vet's?

Knowledge and understanding create security.

A: Think about what you would need to know before a visit to the hospital. What would comfort and reassure you? First, explain to us why we are going well before we leave. Tell us who will be touching us and what will happen to us. For example, picture all of the following as if you were seeing it yourself as you explain that we are going to be neutered. Explain that we will be put under anesthesia for a time so that we will not feel the pain of the operation. Tell us that the doctor will shave us, make an incision, and remove our testicles so that we cannot reproduce. Tell us that after the testicles have been removed, the doctor will stitch us up and we will be put in a soft, warm, comfortable spot to wake up and begin recovering. Tell us that the stitches may itch, but we must leave them alone as best we can. Tell us that you will soon come to pick us up and go home. Tell us that you know we'll come through the operation with flying colors and heal rapidly and feel great! Picture us happy, healthy, and running around with joy.

You need to know that by picturing what will happen while you are explaining things to us, we are much better able to understand what you are telling us. By explaining to us what will be happening, you give us what to expect and time to prepare. This will help us eliminate fear of the unknown.

By telling us how you wish us to handle the stitches, for instance, you show us another way to heal. Normally we'd lick a wound to help it heal, but if you explain to us that there is another way, many of us will try to honor your way.

By picturing and telling us that we will be fine, you show us that we will be okay and help us hold onto that picture instead of focusing on our fear or pain. You clearly communicate that you believe we will do great and normally we do!

When we are under anesthesia, we are totally aware of everything that's happening to us. We remember most of the experience once we come out of anesthesia as well. Feeling helpless and unable to control our own bodies while under anesthesia is a terrifying experience for some of us. Some of us remain confused or not fully in our bodies for hours or days after the operation. The anesthesia is a powerful chemical, and many of us are sensitive to it and will need help clearing it out of our systems.

When we're in for a vet examination, stay with us, if you can. The table and the room are often cold physically and emotionally. Often we sense what happened in the room to the animal before us. Help us feel calm and secure by touching or holding us and speaking gently. If we must remain at the clinic without you, please leave us something familiar, like an old tee shirt you have worn recently. Tell us when you will return and come get us as quickly as possible.

How do you feel about being neutered?

Most of us have accepted neutering as part of living in human society.

A: It would be wonderful if we could have more control over our own procreation. Unfortunately for most of us, our instincts overpower our higher consciousness when we smell a bitch in season. Some of us are able to maintain self-control and we are very proud of this ability. Again, individual dogs handle the responsibility of remaining fertile differently than others. Some of us are controlled by our hormones and neutering allows us to focus on our mission with our people more easily. We recognize that overpopulation is a problem for us in human society. We need to work together so that all dogs and humans live happy, healthy lives.

Many female dogs love to be mothers. Others choose to dedicate their lives to their human families. Those of us who wish to be mothers, wish to provide our puppies with the same gifts human mothers wish to provide their children—a healthy start in life, a safe environment to grow up in, a happy home, and a purpose in life. If these things are not possible for each and every puppy, then we happily accept neutering. We do not like to breed with a mate we have not chosen ourselves. We prefer to choose our own mates in order to produce the healthiest, most balanced offspring. Many unhealthy, unbalanced dogs have come into life as the result of humans deciding which dog to breed to another. Often your criteria does not match ours. On the other hand, conscientious humans can help us by offering us good partners, but letting us, the two dogs together make the final decision. When a person respects us as individuals, they will take into account our personal needs and desires and do their best to act for our highest good and the highest good of our offspring.

Neutering is a big decision. You need to consider many factors before doing it. Please talk with us about it and explain why you wish us to be neutered, as well as when and how it will happen. Allow us to prepare for it. Be sure that we are healthy and strong before the operation and please do not compromise our systems before the operation with vaccinations or other drugs. Give us time to heal, with lots of love, fresh water, and good food.

What do you think about fleas?

Fleas are fellow creatures whose job is to help bring a body into balance.

A: Fleas are not vermin. They are not the enemy. We've had a long relationship with fleas, parasites, mites, flies. These beings live on us and are with us much of the time. When we are infested with bugs, it means that our bodies are out of balance and sick. The fleas are just doing their job, helping to right an imbalance. A dog with a bad case of fleas either builds a stronger system or gets sicker and eventually dies. Poisoning fleas is a losing battle and usually poisons us much more effectively than it does them. The best defense against a parasite infestation is a healthy, happy body.

What is it like for you
to go blind or deaf or lose the
use of a leg?

*We cope by accepting
and compensating.*

A: Again, we have a different attitude towards these experiences than most humans. Losing our eyesight is the least traumatic for most of us because we are used to seeing with our other senses in combination with our eyes. When we are little puppies, our eyesight is the last sense we develop. From birth we depend on our noses and higher sense of smell to introduce us to the physical world. Taste, touch, hearing, and learning to distinguish between our energetic body and our physical body is how we first experience the world. Eyesight is a kind of icing on the cake. We really appreciate it, but don't depend on it. If we lose our eyesight from illness or injury, we compensate with our other senses and our third or non-physical eye.

Deafness is tougher on us because hearing is important for carrying out our sense of duty as watchdogs. Also our ears are always on, even when we sleep. When we lose our hearing, we feel more vulnerable, especially during sleep. We do our best to compensate, and many of us do so well with our other senses that you may not realize our deafness for quite a while.

Losing a leg is not the end of the world. Again, we compensate by shifting our weight onto the other legs. After a time, our bodies will develop structural imbalances. Your conscious touch, massaging and releasing tension, spinal adjustments, and anything that keeps the energy flowing through our bodies is extremely helpful when we have lost a leg. The more you do these things, the longer we will remain comfortable and active. Sometimes, if we have been an active working or herding dog, we will need your encouragement while we adjust to three legs. Don't feel sorry for us. Support us with joy and love and we will come into balance rapidly.

Lastly, we do not dwell on the loss of something. We focus on what we have, not on what we don't have.

How do you feel about euthanasia?

Choose euthanasia out of compassion.

A: Euthanasia is often just a way to dispose of us. When our lives and missions are aborted in this way, it is emotionally and spiritually painful to us. But sometimes euthanasia is a viable and helpful option. Sometimes, especially after fighting a lingering illness, it is difficult for us to let go. Euthanasia, when given with compassion and tenderness, can be a gift.

Your attitude and energy around the moment of euthanasia is key. If you feel guilty, miserable, full of pity, angry, or out of touch, our final experience will very likely match your feelings. These emotions carry a vibration that is vastly different from love, compassion, peace, and support. At the moment of death, our soul is imprinted with the last emotions we experience. If you are near us, sending us love, telling us to return to the arms of God, to Peace, to the Light, we will leave our bodies in a beautiful way. This is what our souls will remember of our last moments and we will feel content.

Choose euthanasia for us out of compassion. Listen to your own hearts to know when your beloved friends are telling you we are ready to go. Be with us when it happens. Trust that we are returning to Love. Trust that we will be separated physically only, and that our souls, once joined in love, will never be apart.

If you are involved in euthanizing dogs you haven't had time to get to know, the same directions apply. Remember that this dog about to die is someone's beloved friend (or wanted to be), and treat her with gentle compassion as you would any beloved family member.

How can we make animal shelters better for you?

Comfort on all levels.

A: Each of us has different needs but the most important thing is the attitudes of the humans who care for us. The humans around us set the tone that creates relative comfort or triggers our fear and stress. Physical comfort includes warmth, privacy, companionship of other dogs, play time, fresh air, sunlight, and an area for play and elimination that is separate from our sleeping quarters. The more isolated animals are in the space, the greater the stress. Fewer dogs together in small group areas is usually better than lots of dogs in individual cages in close quarters. Remember that we normally live in packs, which means six or eight animals, not sixty. Companionship is important.

aring for the senses and the *mind*

chapter nine

"*I am the rug beneath your feet that buffers you from all the harshness of life.*"

—Dog

Why is it harder to lose a dear canine friend than a human friend or relative?

We bring you simple, uncluttered, unfettered love.

A: Most humans cannot yet live this way. Don't worry about why your human friends and relatives aren't as dear to you as we are. Ask yourself, "Can I be as dear to others as their dogs are to them?" The key is not to wait for people to change. The key is to choose today to begin loving like a dog. Each human in your life longs for love. If you simplify your love, release your ego and embrace joy, other people in your life will find you as lovable as a dog. If every human tried this, even for a few hours or a day, oh what a world it would be! Ahhhh, then we will have really accomplished something!

Have you been with me
before? Will you return?

*Many of us have been with our
beloved human beings
through many lifetimes.*

A: Sometimes we die and return to you in your present lifetime. Once we have bonded together in love, nothing can
keep us apart. Lifetime to lifetime, wherever our souls travel, if we agree to come together in physical form we will.
Often, we will return to you during a particularly challenging time, only to leave you when you have passed through
it. Sometimes we will stay with you for a long time.
Sometimes our job is completed in a short time. When you
really learn that we are, all of us—dogs and people alike—
only in a physical form for brief periods, and that we all
choose to come and go at particular times, you will appreciate the bigger picture.

Do you choose the people you want to be with or is it determined in the other realm?

Usually the soul decides.

A: Either we make an agreement at the soul level with a person, or we just decide to take our chances and go where life leads us—preferably to a person who needs us and will appreciate and care for us. The agreement to be together between a human soul and a canine soul can take place on this side or on the other. It doesn't matter as souls know no boundaries.

What do you dream about?

Lots of things.

A: We usually dream of fun, physical activities. It's our way of reconnecting to joy. Often we run, chase rabbits, sheep, balls, or other toys in our dreams. When we're older, we dream about the beautiful things we've experienced in our lives with you. We dream that we are young and full of life. Sometimes we dream about our place at the feet of God. We reconnect with the Creator, unencumbered by a body, to bask in the glory of Divine Love. This is a recharging experience. Often when we sit at the feet of God in our dreams we're asking for help or guidance. We never hesitate to go straight to the top to get whatever we need.

How can you find me if we are separated by hundreds or thousands of miles?

Love, that's how!

A: When we truly love a human and know that they love us in return, an energetic link bonds us forever. This love becomes a kind of cord connecting us to our person. This cord is not even severed in death. Our souls will be linked forever. When you think that death, the "Grand Separation," as most humans think of it, cannot keep us apart, what's a couple thousand miles?

But how does that work?

Humans have the most difficult time accepting simple things.

A: The energy field of every living organism holds memory. This memory has power beyond space and time, beyond physical reality. Once we've bonded to a human, and they to us, each of us holds the memory or energetic signature of the other within our own energy fields. If we are separated, our memory of this beautiful shared love will cause us to search for reunification, to complete the bond again. It's a magnetic response. Once we have begun the quest, we can hardly stop. We've turned on our radar and will only stop when we've found our way home to you again.

We engage all of our senses to accomplish the task. We use our hearing, sight, noses, but also our inner hearing, sight and smell. Our inner senses connect us with the Divine. You sometimes call this ability the "sixth" sense. When we engage our inner senses, there is no separation, no distance, no space, no time. We find you. It's really very simple.

We know that you can sense earthquakes before they happen. *How* do you do this?

We feel the vibrational shifts.

A: Our auras are antennae—like when we wish them to be. Just as we sense a vibrational shift in your energy field with the signature of an epileptic seizure, we can feel the vibrational shift in the air, in the soil, in the plants and trees before an earthquake. You can remember how to tune in to this sense as well. You have the ability to sense auras, vibrational shifts, all of it, just as we do. You just have to train yourself to pay attention and see with more of yourself. Your eyes, ears, and skin are only half of what you have at your disposal.

Do you see human auras?

Yes, we see, smell, and feel your energy fields or auras.

A: When we look at you, using all our senses, we perceive an energy field around your physical body. In fact, we can't see you without it! It's as clear to us as your arms and legs. We perceive the aura or energy fields of all living things. Our ancestors developed both the ability to perceive the energy fields of the animals we hunted and our use of our own personal energy fields for accomplishing different things. For example, when a wolf is hunting a rabbit, she consciously pulls her energy field in close to her body, making its vibration calm and quiet. When she comes within range of the rabbit, she throws her energy field out like a net, surrounding the rabbit. The rabbit senses the wolf's energy field and for a fraction of a second is confused about where the wolf is coming from.

Usually the rabbit's own energy field acts like an antenna, picking up on signals sent out by the energy fields of predators. In this respect, the rabbit actually has the advantage, because their antenna-like energy fields often give them plenty of warning about dangers in the vicinity. This is why a predator fails as often as eight out of ten tries to catch their prey.

Wolves and others from our dog family can also extend their aura energy fields well beyond our bodies to signal others in our family, or our competitors, that we own this territory. When we meet each other, our first contact is through our energy fields. We first check each other out, aura to aura. Then we decide if we are comfortable or not with each other, depending how our energy fields match up. If we are comfortable with each other, we will make friendly gestures. If we are uncomfortable, we will posture or attack, depending on how serious a threat we perceive the other to be.

With human beings, we see a great deal in the aura or energy field. You carry an energetic signature of your true nature in your aura. You may be able to hide your true natures from each other, through smoke screens of talk or fancy clothes, but you cannot hide your true natures from us. This is why many of you have learned that if we don't like a person, there's a very good reason to be careful in your relationship with them.

Can you tell if a human could have future health problems by observing their aura?

Yes.

A: Often we can because physical, emotional, mental, and spiritual disease appears in the aura or energy field before it manifests in the physical body. Often we are aware before you are that an illness or disease is on the way. For instance, we can sense that a person is about to have an epileptic seizure before it happens because an epileptic seizure appears first as a particular vibrational shift in the person's aura. Some of us are more sensitive to this than others, but most of us can remember how to do this if we know it's important to you. We just need to create a clear communication set of signals between us. We first need to know that you wish us to pay attention and to alert you to changes in your auras. Tell us how you want us to communicate to you that a problem is forming. Show us how you will respond to our signal. Acknowledge that you have understood and acted upon our communication.

Do you miss the past? Do you think about the future?

We do our best to find joy wherever we are.

A: If you are asking do we long for something that is no longer in our lives, the answer is "sometimes." If we lose a person, we do our best to find them. If that isn't possible, we will try to connect with another person to love.

Do we miss the activities of the past? We do, sometimes. Usually we do our best to find joy wherever we are. As we mentioned before, if the activities of the past were fulfilling and satisfying, as in doing a job like herding sheep, and that job or activity is no longer available, we will need help adjusting. We will need a new job to replace the old.

If we are with the person we love, then most of the time the past doesn't matter. The present is everything!

We guess you'd say the future is irrelevant for us. The present moment is everything! It's hard to have regrets when we are living fully in the present.

what do you teach us about spirit?

chapter ten

"Out of his great heart beams such warmth that we can feel it in our own hearts whenever we choose. Within such warmth, our own wings start to sprout a little."

—Sarah M. Irvine from "Angel Dog"

Do you have spiritual intuition, and does the same God that works through all people work through you?

We are all one.

A: This book is all about contacting our spiritual intuition, as you call it, or our Divine Consciousness, as we prefer to describe it. Every being on the planet has Divine Consciousness. Each being expresses their Divine Consciousness in their own unique way.

Yes, the same god that works through people works through us. We are all one, there is no otherness, no separation, physical or spiritual, between species. In order to experience individuality, you have created a perception of separateness. Although it is difficult to comprehend, the two are not synonymous.

What is life all about?

Life is about joy.

A: If you're not having fun, what is the point? Joy is a state of mind and body. We cannot be happy in mind if our bodies are not happy. Fun is a relative term. For us fun is play and meaningful work combined every moment of every day. By meaningful work, we mean doing something that supports the humans we love. Sometimes this means herding sheep, hunting foxes, guarding the house. Other times it means being with the person we share our lives with and showering them with love in every way we can. Giving and receiving love gives us the greatest joy of all. This is what life is all about for us.

It's important to decide what is fun and meaningful for each of us, personally. Life is short, so make everything as joyful as possible.

Where do you go when you die?

The Place of Reunification.

A: Death is not the end of the soul but only the end of this particular body. We know that death is temporary. Here is what happens: A body (all physical bodies—human, canine, spider) breaks down and no longer functions. The soul leaves the body and evaporates into the air. As it evaporates, the energy changes again, rejoining Life. By Life we mean endless life, everlasting life, unity with Love, with the Creator. Some of you call this "heaven." Some of you call it "the hereafter." We call it the "Place of Reunification." Here there is no physical pain or suffering. Here the soul sees clearly, unconfined by physical form and personal experience. Here the soul gains perspective on her life this time around. The soul has the opportunity to review this last life and decide what to do next.

Yes, dogs have souls. Our souls are capable of free will, just like yours are. We can choose to return to a new body and life experience or we can choose to remain in spirit. At this time there is a major difference between the human soul's journey and the dog's. We remember our past life-times. Most of you do not. We aren't sure why this is. The Creator must have a good reason for this. We are very happy to remember what we worked on or experienced in our previous lifetimes. We are happy that we see the bigger picture. Seeing the bigger picture allows us to be much less attached to our bodies and particular life experiences than most of you are. We don't dwell on what we did or didn't do. We focus more on our mission and the joy of being alive. Perhaps we can be more fully in the present moment than you can be because we understand that life goes on and on and on. Past pains, mistakes, or misunderstandings are not the end of the world. There is always time to choose kindness. There is always time to play.

Can you visit with me once you are spirit?

All the time.

A: Of course. We visit you all the time when we are in spirit. You don't see us because you don't believe that you can. Sometimes you do see us or feel our presence soon after we die. Many of you have had the experience of feeling us at the foot of the bed or seeing us out of the corner of your eye, or hearing us scratch at the door to come in. These are real experiences, as real as physical experience, even though your rational minds try to tell you differently. In your longing for us, you break through your rational disbelief and conditioning to allow yourself to experience our loving presence after we have left our bodies behind.

After your death, I dreamt that you came to me. *Was* this wishful thinking or did you really come to me?

We really do come to you in your dreams.

A: When humans dream, their minds no longer control, judge, or distort. Your dream state is pure. When you wake up you often recall your dreams through the filter of your mind and your mind may distort the truth. However, when you relax your body and mind in sleep and enter into the dream time, you reconnect to the reality we all share. While you dream, you have the opportunity to receive messages, guidance, divine inspiration. Becoming more connected to your own personal dream process will empower you to communicate with us, as well as with your higher self, angels, and with God. You can remember who you truly are by becoming consciously aware of your dream state and by using it as a stepping stone to your true, authentic, divine nature. Once you connect to your true self, you will feel no separation, no loss, no grief.

We often come to you in your dreams after we have died in order to reassure you that we are well, beautiful, ecstatically happy. Even though in your dream, you might see us in familiar surroundings, you are actually seeing us in heaven, the place of Oneness, of Connection to All-That-Is. Here there is no pain, no suffering, no sadness. The setting is not as important as the feeling of joy and wholeness which we convey to you in the dream. This is the purpose of coming to you in your dreams.

Do you miss being in a body on earth?

Sometimes yes, sometimes no.

A: It depends on many different factors. If we have had a difficult or painful life, being in spirit is much better. If we have had a fulfilling life, then leaving our bodies is just closing a door on a job well done. There are no regrets, although there is often sadness because you feel that we are leaving you for good. This is an incorrect but powerful belief system held deeply in the cells of most of you. A body is simply a temporary home for the soul. We try to use it well, enjoying all the gifts and opportunities it provides us. Of course, if we are not finished with our work or individual mission, then we try to return to a new body as soon as possible to complete what we started.

Remember, we know that a body is temporary and we remember our past lives. We know that leaving our bodies to reconnect to God is a glorious experience, just as returning to earth to experience a new life can be glorious, even with all its risks. Journeying through life and death, and life and death again and again, is a wonderful way to learn, to grow and be of service to humankind, to the Earth and all her creatures and to God.

119

How much do you remember from your past lives?

A great deal, usually.

A: Some of us can recall dozens at a time, some can recall only a particular one. It depends on how many we've had as well as how important it is for us to remember. Usually we focus on those lives that are deeply affecting our present lifetime. For example, if we have spent lifetimes with one person, you, we'll be conscious of your journey as well as our own with you. We'll often remember your soul's purpose, even when you can't remember. Often we're with you to remind you of your purpose. Some of us go to great lengths to get you back on track if you've lost your way. It gives us great joy to help you remember who you really are!

What can survivors do to help you if your human guardian dies before you do?

We need love and support, just as people do.

A: Losing the person we love is very difficult for us. We grieve just as you do. It's important to tell us that they're gone and that they will not return to us as we knew them. Most of us know this on a spiritual level, but when we're very involved in physical activity with our person, some of us might have a hard time letting go and accepting the fact that our human guardian is gone and will not return.

We need lots of love, support and quiet time, just as other family members do. We often benefit from a reassignment—a new person to love and care for. If the person we love has time to speak to us about this before they die, it can help a great deal. If our person asks us to take care of another person before they die, usually we will make this transition to a new guardian much more easily. In the case of a sudden death of a guardian, his family can help us by caring for us and remembering that we are grieving, just as they are.

If you have an ill or elderly family member with a devoted dog, know that the dog is helping that person in immeasurable ways. We help ease pain and anchor the person in love even in the midst of drugs and mental or physical incapacity. You may not be able to see what we are doing, but our person knows it at a soul level, if not on a conscious level. What a shame it is that beloved friends such as this are often ignored, mistreated, and even taken to the shelter after the death of the person they have helped so much. Please make a plan for what will happen to us after such a death, just as you would for a child. Please don't just throw us away.

Do you believe in angels?

We have a great deal in common with angels.

A: Of course! We sense, see, smell, hear, and feel angels working with humans, angels working with plants, and angels working with other animals. Some of us are angels with four feet and a physical body. It's no accident that angels are drawn to us and that we are drawn to angels. We share an immutable connection to the Divine and a mission to help human beings find their way back to God.

Because we have free will, just as you do, we evolve and grow at a soul level like you. Many people are not aware of the suffering of other humans and animals. Most people cannot hear the Earth cry or laugh. The important thing is that you believe you are aware. Now you can choose to do something with this awareness, to make a positive difference. What will it be?

Do canines have a religion?

We have a spiritual practice.

A: If you're asking, do we have a spiritual practice? Then yes, we do. It's love and compassion, joy, and being fully present in the moment. It's treating everyone with honor and seeing the best in everybody.

We humans often have a hard time following those principles. *Do* you ever have difficulties?

Yes, we do.

A: If we have been mistreated, abandoned, or if we have failed or disappointed someone, we can often stray from our path, just as you do. Usually, receiving love and compassion from a human being or another animal will get us back on track. You see, we always want to return to the Light, to goodness and wholeness. Sometimes we get lost, mentally or emotionally, and need support to help us find the way home. We never choose to be angry or cruel, but fear and confusion can cause us to respond in these ways. Again, love and kindness are the very best medicines.

Why is it so difficult for most of us to offer unconditional forgiveness and love? it seems to come to you so easily!

You have ego. We don't.

A: There are many faces of human ego. Sometimes it is expressed as an air of superiority. Sometimes it is expressed as withholding. Sometimes it is expressed as sacrifice or martyrdom. Sometimes it is expressed as victimhood. All of these expressions of ego create separation and duality—the illusion that you and the other have no common bonds. Only humans who have really understood how their own egos create separation can express and give unconditional love and forgiveness.

Can you reincarnate as a cat, bird, or other animal, a tree, or a human?

We are beings of free will, as you are.

A: It depends on the personal awareness level of the individual dog. If we choose to come back as something other than dog, we can. However, there is a group of souls suited to be canines, just as there is a group of souls suited to be human. Choosing to come back as a different animal would be choosing a very different life path. While this would be challenging, it is not impossible if one soul really desires to do so.

What is the key to truly seeing the full potential of every human being as you do?

A: Compassion and understanding. Patience and trust.

How do you see the future of dog and human interactions?

We are all in this together.

A: This time of change is about integration, cooperation, and intuition. It is about the blending of two beings, two energies into one. There is an energy of togetherness, peace, cooperation, the opportunity to merge into the oneness that is streaming into the planet at this time. You can see this in its opposite—wars based on religious, racial, and cultural differences. However, at this moment in time, each human being is being supported to choose unity and love over separateness. Each of you, throughout the days ahead, will have the opportunity to choose oneness over otherness. Look at each situation and ask yourself how you wish to respond. Do you choose anger and blaming another or do you try to see things from the other's point of view and do something to find a peaceful solution and create togetherness? Are you afraid? You have tremendous support at this time to choose love over fear, but it's up to you to make a loving action versus a fear-based action.

We are optimistic that all of us on Earth are on the brink of a new awakening. We deeply believe that we will become closer and understand each other at last. As animals, we relate to other animals in physical and non-physical ways. We can tune into each other's Divine Consciousness or choose to remain in the physical, more limited self. When human beings remember that you can do this too, the whole planet will make a giant leap in its evolution. We're all in this together. Every being affects all the other beings on the planet. As each of you remembers that you are divine beings, just as each dog, cat, horse, spider, worm, whale, fish, flower, blade of grass is, everything will change.

We are delighted and honored to have helped you come this far. We are really excited about what's coming.

Thank you for asking.

in the company of *Dogs*

This book has been a labor of love—for all the dogs I've met and for all the people who have ever loved or been loved by a dog. The generosity of the canine with their unconditional loyalty and devotion continues to touch and inspire me. As I re-read the dogs' answers and insights, I get something new each time. Extraordinary beings.

The Council of Dogs has this to say to you at this time:

"Beloveds, you are our great joy. You give us so much of yourselves and we, lucky we, get to give you our hearts, our love and devotion. Always will we be by your side, as long as the Creator allows for our destinies are inexplicably linked. We are true friends until the end of time. We love you!"

May you return to this book over and over as you journey through your life in the company of dogs. And to paraphrase a wonderful bumper sticker, "May we all be the people our dogs think we are!"

about
The Author

KATE SOLISTI-MATTELON, internationally-known speaker, author and teacher, is a professional animal communicator. Since 1992, she has worked with individual animal guardians, holistic veterinarians, trainers and other professionals assisting in solving behavioral problems, understanding health problems, healing past traumas, and facilitating understanding between humans and animals. Kate has conducted classes, seminars and workshops throughout the United States and Europe.

Kate has contributed articles to *Animal Wellness, Tiger Tribe, Wolf Clan, Best Friends* and *Species Link* magazines. Kate is the author of several books on animal communication and holistic health. Kate's work with animals has been featured in numerous books, journals and newspapers. She is an expert in dog nutrition and with her husband, Patrice Mattelon, has produced a video, *"Save Your Dog! Nourish Him the Way He's Built to Eat."* Kate and Patrice teach canine nutrition and Bach Flower Remedies for dogs at the Lang Institute of Canine Massage in Loveland, Colorado.

To learn more about Kate, or to schedule a personal consultation visit her website:

www.AKinshipwithAnimals.com

about
Council Oak Books

Since 1984 Council Oak Books has published books from all over the world, books that cross cultural lines to bring new understanding. Drawing from history, we publish for the future, presenting books that point the way to a richer life and a better world. Council Oak Books takes its name from a great oak tree, sacred to the Creek Indians, that still grows in the center of Tulsa, our home city. Our books are meant to inspire the sharing of knowledge in the quiet, contemplative space beneath the great Oak.

In keeping with this mission, we publish books on alternative health for animals, as well as the spiritual bond between humans and animals and other innovative titles on the relationship between humans and nature.

Please visit our website for a complete list of our current titles:

www.counciloakbooks.com

unconditional love

devotion

acceptance

loyalty

Ceal & Dan Moran
273 Natures Way
Charlotte, VT 05445